BRANCH LINE TO SOUTHWOLD

Vic Mitchell and Keith Smith

Cover design – Deborah Goodridge

First published 1984   Reprinted 1987

ISBN 0 906520 15 0

© Middleton Press, 1984

Typeset by CitySet - Bosham 573270

*Published by Middleton Press
          Easebourne Lane
          Midhurst, West Sussex
          GU29 9AZ
          073 081 3169*

*Printed & bound by Biddles Ltd,
          Guildford and Kings Lynn*

INDEX

ACKNOWLEDGMENTS

We are most grateful for the assistance received from the individuals and organisations recorded in the photograph caption credits and also to the West Sussex Library Service. Our thanks also go to C.R. Gordon Stuart for providing most of the tickets and to Mrs. E. Fisk, Mrs. B. Mitchell and N. Stanyon for proof reading. We are also grateful to M. Seymour for information obtained from the Ffestiniog Railway Archives.

AUTHOR'S NOTES

The photographs are arranged, as far as possible, in geographical order, from west to east, and in chronological order at each location. The handbills, advertisements and station headings are reproduced from the Company's 1914 timetable booklet. The station drawings were produced in 1894 on behalf of the Great Eastern Railway, to the scale of 3mm to 1 foot. The drawings of the locomotives and the rolling stock are also to that scale.

GEOGRAPHICAL SETTING

The railway ran throughout its length in the broad shallow valley of the River Blyth. At its seaward end the valley broadens into wide expanses of marsh whilst above the first road bridge over the river, at Blythburgh (over three miles inland), it bears fertile agricultural land. In the mid-eighteenth century the river was rendered navigable up to Halesworth by the provision of a short length of canal and several locks. The underlying sand and, in places, gravel is visible today at a number of quarries. The atmosphere of the district was eloquently described by E.S. Tonk in his history of the line when recounting a journey from Halesworth –

"The porters loaded the luggage into the vans, everyone clambered leisurely aboard and, with a shrill squeak from the engine, the train moved off for its journey through the meadows and flower-starred marshes; the "regulars" would foregather in the guard's special compartment, holier than the little-used firsts, to chat about local affairs, the familiar landscape forgotten; but to the holiday passenger the rocking carriage brought many unexpected sights of nature, which pressed closely on the railway. Brambles and honeysuckle brushed the windows, to give way near Wenhaston to vegetation indicative of moister conditions – willows, alders and reed-filled ditches; the best part of the trip, perhaps, was between Blythburgh and Walberswick, where could be seen herons fishing in the shallows (they still nest at Hill Crest) and unfamiliar species of duck as well as the ubiquitous moorhen."

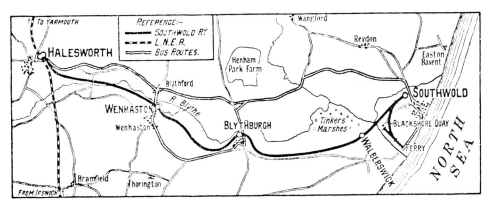

(Railway Magazine)

HISTORICAL BACKGROUND

During the 1850s the main line of the East Suffolk Railway, through Halesworth, was completed, becoming incorporated into the Great Eastern Railway in 1862. Local requests for a branch line to be built to Southwold were unsuccessful and so a public meeting in 1875 resolved that a narrow gauge railway should be constructed to the coastal resort and small port of Southwold, whose development was being restricted by lack of connection to the national railway system. Local entrepreneurs formed a company which secured an Act of Parliament in July 1876 for its construction but then failed to raise sufficient funds for contracts to be let. Outsiders eventually took control and work started in May 1878, with rails coming from South Wales and sleepers from Norway, direct to Southwold Harbour. The line was opened on 24th September 1879 and was soon a success. It initially had only one intermediate station, at Wenhaston. There were no continuous brakes and so the Board of Trade imposed a speed limit of 16 mph. The company's first locomotive foreman had previously served on a Chinese narrow gauge line and its second was from an equally unusual West Sussex railway, described in our *Branch Line to Selsey*.

The coming of the railway probably brought about more change to the town of Southwold than any other single event in its history. An increase in house building coincided with the steady development of the area as a holiday resort. Perishable commodities such as fish and dairy products could be speedily sent by rail to urban markets and newspapers, mail and a greater variety of general merchandise and foodstuffs could be brought into the district more easily. By the turn of the century, more than 100,000 passengers were carried annually, together with around 9000 tons of minerals (mainly coal) and 6000 tons of other goods traffic. The Edwardian heyday can be seen in many of the photographs in the following pages.

The company decided to convert its line to standard gauge and in the period 1906-08 widened several bridges at the Halesworth end and also the swing bridge. This was part of a scheme to modernise and extend operations to Lowestoft but it failed, due to lack of finance.

In mediaeval times Southwold had been an important port but had steadily declined due to the loss of a protecting arm of land and steady silting of the river mouth. At the end of the nineteenth century Lowestoft and Yarmouth were becoming heavily congested with boats of the herring fleet and so a proposal to reinvigorate Southwold harbour was made.

Great antagonism existed between the Harbour Commissioners and the Railway Company, as they were in competition for the small freight traffic to the town. It took nearly ten years of legal wrangling before a one-mile long branch line was opened to the harbour in October 1914, by which time the fishing crisis had passed. The junction, near the bridge, allowed trains to run directly to and from Southwold only. The branch had a trailing connection onto Blackshore Quay and carried little traffic, except sea defence material.

World War I brought a decline in tourist traffic but movement of troops largely compensated for this. The War Department took control of the line for the war years, during which time it suffered bomb damage from an airship raid. The WD did not relinquish control until August 1921.

1926 was the first year in which the company made a loss, and it was "the beginning of the end". It was due to competition from road transport, particularly from the buses which had become more frequent and had the advantage of operating into the centres of the populated areas.

1927 showed a small profit of £751 but the downward trend in passenger figures continued, despite massive fare reductions. Wages and salaries were also reduced. No financial assistance was available from any source.

The last passenger train ran on 11th April 1929. Final freight movements took place during the following week and the last day on which an engine was in steam was 20th April.

The following year two rival revival schemes were launched. Mr. Belcher, formerly the locomotive foreman, proposed relaying the track to standard gauge and extending it to connect with the incomplete Mid-Suffolk Light Railway. Mr. Ronald Shephard, a self-styled light railway engineer, advocated retaining the narrow gauge and the use of special wagons on which standard gauge wagons could be carried fully laden,

avoiding the need for transhipment at Halesworth. Petrol railcars were proposed for passengers. Both schemes failed but Mr. Shephard resurrected his proposals in 1941, this time supported by Southwold Corporation, and a detailed Memorandum was presented to the Minister of War Transport. He now proposed conversion to standard gauge and the hire of Sentinel locomotives from the LNER. Much of the railway equipment had already been removed and most of the remainder went by the end of the year. The legal problems which had laid the railway dormant for 12 years were brushed aside by the urgent war-time need for steel. The minimal fuel savings that the reopening of the railway would have brought about were ignored by the Minister, who had matters of greater importance to deal with at that time.

The legal death of the company has been very protracted. In 1960 it was registered as a limited company and the Liquidator appointed solicitors, who have had to disclaim some areas of land claimed by squatters. Although the company still exists all saleable property has been disposed of and it is now virtually wound up.

In its early years, the railway had been a model of desirable and efficient local transport but after World War I it became just the reverse. It was the subject of a set of 12 comic postcards, which went as far as caricaturing the staff. Some of them are reproduced herein.

The gauge of 3 ft was unusual for an English passenger line, although common on Irish and Manx railways.

TRAIN SERVICES

It appears that initially there were four journeys daily but this was soon increased to five. By 1910, this extra train only operated on Saturdays and the Sunday service was withdrawn, being reinstated the following year with two return journeys. In 1914, there were four trains on weekdays only, with an extra train every evening during June and on Mondays, Fridays and Saturdays during May. Special leave trains were run on Saturday and Sunday evenings during World War I for troops stationed near Blythburgh. During the 1920s, there were normally four return journeys, operated during a 12-hour working day, weekdays only, with an additional train on Saturday evenings in the summer months only. In the early 1920s, the evening service operated daily during the summer. During the later years of the line, the timetable allowed for a permissively worked freight trip to run from Halesworth at about 11.15 am returning from Southwold about an hour later, with a maximum of 14 wagons.

ACCIDENTS

The only fatal accidents to occur both involved employees. The first was at Walberswick in 1883 when the 17-year-old in charge of the station died boarding a moving train.

Near disaster occurred on August Bank Holiday Monday, 1899, when a heavily laden six-coach train stalled on the rising gradient approaching Halesworth at about 8 pm. It was decided to split the train; take three coaches into the station and return for the others. Unfortunately, the latter gravitated back to Wenhaston at considerable speed, but were luckily not derailed on the curves.

On 1st August 1921, two loaded coal wagons broke away from a train between Walberswick and Blythburgh; ran back to the former station and collided with a stationary train.

The second fatality was at Wenhaston, where the station master was mortally injured during shunting operations on Christmas Eve, 1927.

SOUTHWOLD

═ ELECTRIC ═

Picture Palace

YORK ROAD.

THE best and up-to-date Films are used in this Picture Palace, and include Instruction, Humour and Tragedy. Present day events and the stirring episodes in History are shown from time to time. The Palace is also noted for the Excellent Lighting and Steadiness of the Pictures.

CONTINUOUS PERFORMANCE DAILY

From 6.15 o'clock.

:: Complete Change of Programme ::
Mondays, Wednesdays and Fridays.

Prices of Admission: 9d., 6d. and 3d.

School Children are admitted to Saturday Matinees for 1d.

SEASON TICKETS — available — for three months, 16/- & 10/6.

Applications for Hire of Hall should be made to

The Lessee and Manager, R. S. RANSOME.

Three 2–4–0 tank engines were supplied in 1879 by Sharp, Stewart & Co. Ltd of Manchester, however, no. 1 was returned to them in 1883, owing to financial difficulties.

They were painted green, with black and white lining. This was later changed to the Great Eastern Railway style blue, with red lining, the final livery being black.

No. 1 *Southwold*

1. This engine was purchased from Sharp Stewart's Glasgow Works in 1893, as a replacement for the engine returned to them earlier. It was similar to the 2–4–0Ts but had a pair of trailing wheels, a rear coal bunker and an improved cab. It was withdrawn a year before closure and cut up.
(R. Shephard collection)

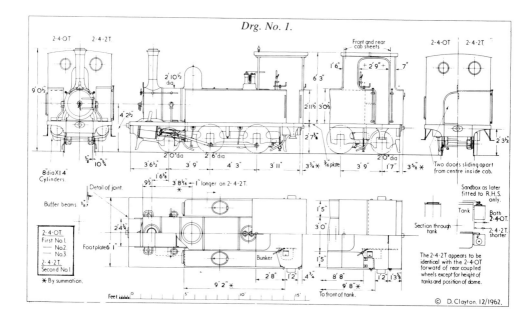

Drg. No. 1.

© D. Clayton. 12/1962.

No. 2 *Halesworth*

2. Photographed in 1911 at Southwold, no. 2 was recorded as having had five new boilers during its career on the line. Like nos. 3 and 4, she was broken up during World War II. (K. Nunn collection/LCGB)

No. 3 *Blyth*

Southwold engines were sometimes sent to Stratford Works for major overhauls and new boilers. No. 3 is seen here at that location on 9th May 1909.
(K. Nunn collection/LCGB)

No. 4 *Wenhaston*

4. In anticipation of heavy traffic on the new harbour branch this 19-ton 0–6–2T was provided by Manning, Wardle & Co. Ltd of Leeds. It retained its own livery of dark green, with light and dark green lining, to the end. It was a powerful, popular locomotive and is seen here leaving Halesworth, near the end of operations. (J.A.G. Coltas)

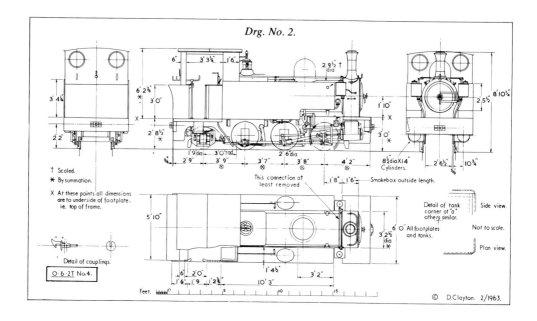

Drg. No. 2.

† Scaled.

∗ By summation.

X At these points all dimensions are to underside of footplate. ie. top of frame.

Detail of couplings.

O·6·2T No.4.

This connection at least removed

Smokebox outside length.

Detail of tank corner at "a" others similar.

6″ O″ All footplates and tanks.

Side view.

Not to scale.

Plan view.

Feet.

© D. Clayton. 2/1963.

5. Six coaches were supplied by the Bristol Wagon Works Co. Ltd. in 1879 in a dark livery. Around 1890, they were repainted cream, with black lettering. Later the lower panels were changed to a red colour. In the Edwardian era, the livery was all maroon, with black lettering, which was eventually altered to white. (R. Shephard collection)

6. All the coaches and 16 of the wagons were built on Cleminson's patented 6-wheeled 'flexible' underframes. Although one wagon of this type survives today on the Ffestiniog Railway, little information is available today about the system.

The outer axles were pivoted and connected by linkages to the centre axle, which was mounted in slides so that it could move sideways on curves. All axles were therefore always on the radius of the curve, reducing rail and flange wear. The design was eclipsed by improvements to the now familiar bogie and was also the cause of the underfloor-groaning, complained of by many passengers. (A.G.W. Garraway)

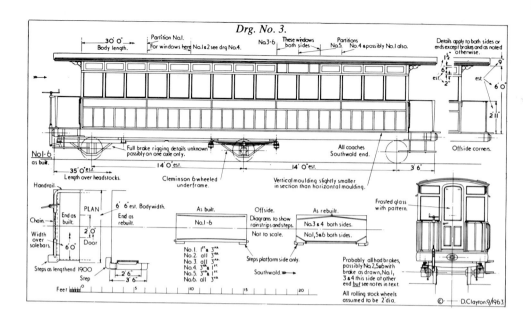

Drg. No. 3.

30' 0" Body length. | Partition No.1. For windows here No.1 & 2 see drg No.4. | No.3-6 | These windows both sides | Partitions No.5. No.4 possibly No.1 also. | Details apply to both sides or ends except brakes and as noted otherwise.

6¼" est. 2" — 9" est. — 6' 0" — 2' 11"

No.1-6 as built.

Full brake rigging details unknown possibly on one axle only.

All coaches Southwold end.

Offside corners.

35' 0" est. Length over headstocks. | 14' 0" est. | 14' 0" est. | 3' 6"

Cleminson 6 wheeled underframe.

Vertical moulding slightly smaller in section than horizontal moulding.

Handrail. | Chain. | End as built. | End as rebuilt. | PLAN | 6' 6" est. Body width. | As built. No.1-6 | Offside. Diagrams to show rainstrips and steps. Not to scale. | As rebuilt. No.3 & 4 both sides. No.1,5 & 6 both sides.

Width over solebars. | 6' 0" | Door | 2' 0"

Steps as length end 1900 | Step | 2' 6" | 3' 6"

Feet

No.1. 1¼" & 3¼"
No.2. all 3¼"
No.3. all 3¼"
No.4. 3¼" & 1¼"
No.5. 3¼" & 1"
No.6. all 3¼"

Steps platform side only.

Southwold →

Frosted glass with pattern.

Probably all had brakes, possibly No.2,5 & 6 with brake as drawn, No.1, 3 & 4 this side at other end but see notes in text.

All rolling stock wheels assumed to be 2' dia.

© — D.Clayton. 9/1963.

Drg. No. 5.

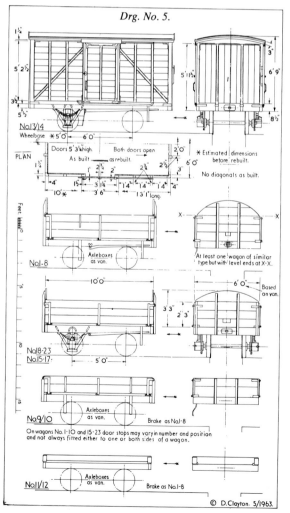

1¼" | 5' 2½" | 3¼" | 5' 5" | 5' 11½" | 6' 9" | 7¾"·3 | 8½"

No.13/14
Wheelbase 5' 0" — 6' 0"

PLAN | Doors 5' 3¾" high. Both doors open. | 2' 0" | * Estimated dimensions before rebuilt.
As built. — as rebuilt. | 1½" | 2¼" | 2" | 2¾" | 2½" | 3" | 6' 0" | No diagonals as built.
1¼" | 4" | 1½" | 3¼" | 1' 4" | 1' 4" | 1' 4" | 4"
10" * | 3' 6" | 13' 1" long.

Feet

No.1-8
Axleboxes as van.

X ————— X

At least one wagon of similar type but with level ends at X-X.

10' 0" | 6' 0" Based on van.
3' 3" | 2' 3"

No.18-23
No.15-17 | 5' 0"

No.9/10
Axleboxes as van. | Brake as No.1-8

On wagons No.1-10 and 15-23 door stops may vary in number and position and not always fitted either to one or both sides of a wagon.

No.11/12
Axleboxes as van. | Brake as No.1-8

© D.Clayton. 5/1963.

The locomotive drawings were compiled from the manufacturer's data whilst the van drawings were made using dimensions from the surviving body. The other rolling stock drawings were made using proportions from the van body, photographs and contemporary sketches. The serious historical modeller concerned about the other numerous changes in detail that occurred whilst the vehicles were in use, should study the photographs contained herein, many of which have come to light since the drawings were made.

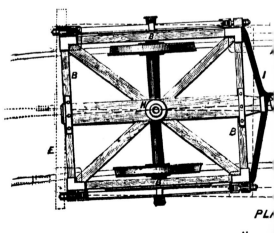

PLA
N

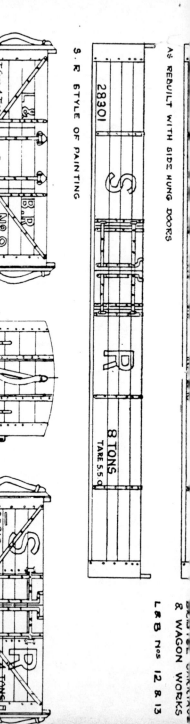

AS REBUILT WITH SIDE HUNG DOORS

S. R. STYLE OF PAINTING

28301

S R

8 TONS
TARE 5.5 C

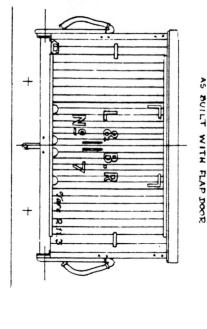

AS BUILT WITH FLAP DOOR

L. & B. R.
Nº 7

To Carry 4 Tons
Tare 2.11.3

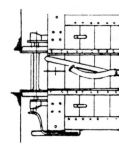

To Carry 4 Tons

L & B R
Nº 9
Tare 2.7.3

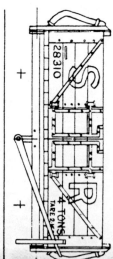

AS REBUILT BY L&BR WITH SIDE HUNG DOORS

28310

S R

4 TONS
TARE 2.

BUILDERS: BRISTOL WAGON & CARRIAGE WORKS

OPEN WAGONS
L & B Nºs 1, 2, 8, 9, 10, 11, 17 & 18
S. Ry Nºs 28304 to 28311

COVERED VANS
L & B Nºs 3, 4, 6, 7, 15 & 16
S. Ry Nºs 47036 to 47041

VACUUM & HAND BRAKES
BRAKE LEVER ONE SIDE ONLY

Drawings courtesy Mr. R. E. Tustin

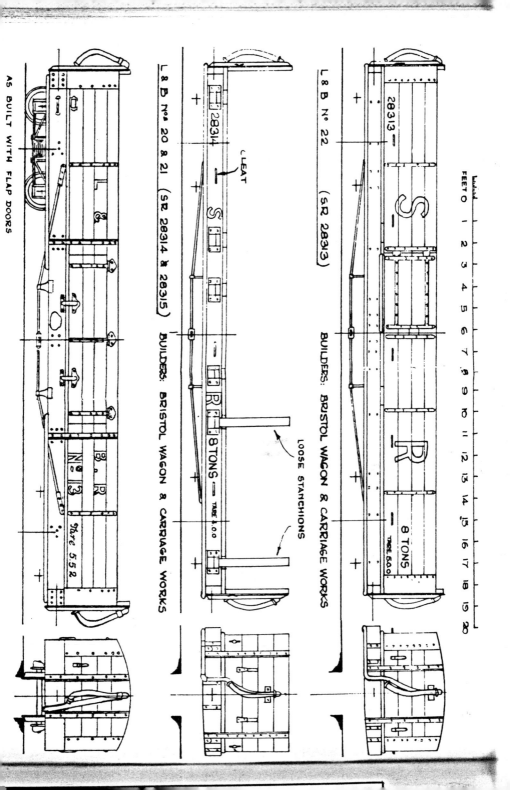

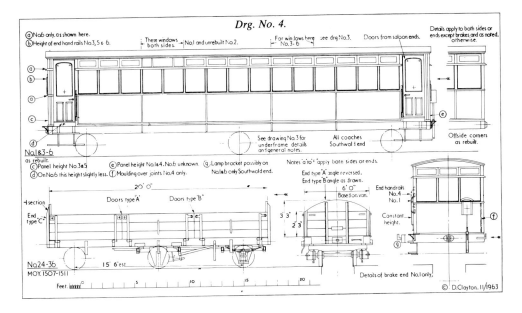

Drg. No. 4.

© D.Clayton. 11/1963

THE ENGINEER. Feb. 15, 1878.

nougn the desirability of using some arrangement of the er carriages of railway rolling stock, by which the axles ld be free to depart from rigid parallelism when traversing ves, has been felt for many years, it is only recently that h has been done in this direction as regards passenger ches in this country. Previously all the stock, and even on most of our lines practically all, was and is fitted with els whose axles are rigidly parallel, a condition which could have been allowed to exist so long, had it not been possible btain the requisite engine power and strength of the parts of vehicles and permanent way which such a system of construc- entails. On a straight line a vehicle with parallel axles y be considered to need very little guidance by the flanges or s; the tendency of such a vehicle in motion is to pursue tinately a straight course, and from it is only caused to art by side pressure on flanges and rails. The intensity of t pressure may be imagined when the amount of skidding ny curve is remembered. For instance, a train passing nd 90 deg. of a curve of, say, ten chains radius, is actually skidded through not less than 60ft. or 70ft., the actual amount of skidding depending, to some extent, upon the length of the vehicles. The Americans first endeavoured in a practical manner to remove this defect by the application of the bogie, but even that very useful invention only partly removes it, as each bogie is in itself a vehicle with parallel axles, but with a short wheel base. It is only recently, however, that even the bogie has been much used in this country, though it has for several years been known that long carriages run much more steadily than those of the ordinary length, and that the proportion of dead weight, or non-paying load, may be made to decrease with increase of length. Car- riages of increased length have been built, most of them running on six wheels with parallel axles, a certain amount of transverse play being allowed in the central axle. Even with this, however, the position of the wheels on a sharp curve is as illustrated in diagram Fig. 4, from which the tendency of the wheels to mount the rails, and the increased power necessary on a curve as compared with a straight line, to pull

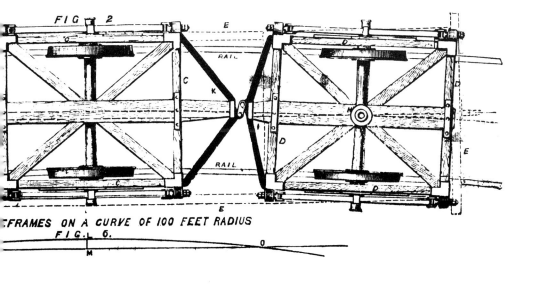

FRAMES ON A CURVE OF 100 FEET RADIUS

such a carriage along, may be estimated. By the use of the bogie the strongest objections to long carriages have been overcome, but others have been imported by which the object of using long carriages has been partly defeated. The bogie car being supported only at or near the ends, its motion is little better than an ordinary short carriage, while the distance between the supports involves the use of very strong and heavy framing, and the bogies of themselves are of such weight that the paying proportion of the load, instead of increasing with the increased length, has in most instances decreased. The parallel axles of the bogies have, moreover, the objections which are attached to short carriages with such axles, so that although it, as far as itself is concerned, permits the construction of long carriages, the grinding and waste of power on curves is as great as with ordinary short carriages, for the direction of pull of the long carriage on a curve causes a thrust on the inner rail at the foremost end and on the outer rail at the rear end.

Our object here is to place before our readers a system of construction invented by Mr. James Cleminson, of Westminster, which overcomes these difficulties in a satisfactory manner, its chief recommendation being that while securing other advantages, it provides the means of passing round the sharpest curves with the axles always normal and radial thereto, whatever its radius, as shown in Fig. 5.

This result is achieved by so attaching the axles to the carriages and to each other as to permit them to adapt themselves automatically and with perfect truth to the varying conformations of a railroad. This is effected as follows :— The axles, with their axle-boxes, guards, and springs, are mounted in frames B C D, Figs. 1 and 2, separate from the main under-frame E. The end frames B and D have central pivots H, around which they swivel freely, whilst the middle frame C is at liberty to slide transversely to the main under-frame E through a range equal to the versed sine L M of an arc N L O, the chord of which equals the wheel-base N M O—see Fig. 6—and finally the frames are connected to each other by the articulated radiating gear I and K. The action of the combination is simply thus :—

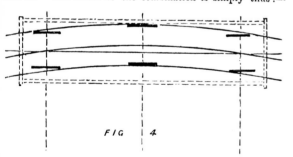

F I G   4

When a vehicle enters a curve, the middle axle and frame C move transversely through the versed sine of the wheel-base arc, and, in doing so, cause the end axles and frames B and D

to swivel around their pivots H, so that all the axles a su positions of radii of the curve.

There is, it will be noticed, nothing of a special natu beyond the axle-frames, required in the application of t invention, either in building new carriages, or converti old stock, these frames entailing very little extra cost, as the main under-frame E is relieved of the strains ordinar due to curves, it is said that it may be reduced in strength

F I G   5

such an extent as to compensate for the cost of the axle-fram All standard fittings, such as axle-boxes, guards, and beari springs, are retained without alteration.

It will be seen that the system permits the construction vehicles of any length, and secures the unattained objects the bogie with the advantage of support throughout the leng of the carriage. In very long carriages, say, 80ft., eig wheels would be employed, with a modification of the arrang ment illustrated. Carriages on the system described have bee running for about a year on the London, Chatham, and Dov Railway, and any passenger travelling from Chatham London will be able to make the journey in the old and ne carriages, and prove for himself the great difference in t comfort of the two systems, especially when travelling by t boat express from Chatham to Herne-hill. The line notoriously crooked, but it is on such lines that the ne carriages show their great superiority in steadiness and smoot ness in running.

Besides being in use on the lines referred to, a number pairs of short Metropolitan carriages are being converted in single long carriages on the new system by splicing, and large quantity of stock is running on the Campanhia Paulis Railway of South America. Several English companies a making up whole trains, and a somewhat remarkable examp of the application of the system is its use on the North Wal Narrow Gauge Railway. The gauge is 1ft. 11½in., and a official trial of a whole new train was recently made at a spee of twenty miles per hour, which on a line which may be almo considered as a continuous set of curves of two chair radius, would be attended with the greatest danger with an other stock.

7. Thomas Moy was not only a coal merchant but built his own wagons in his Peterborough Works. Two arrived soon after the opening; two more in 1896; a batch of six in 1899; a further four in 1914, and finally two second-hand vehicles in 1922. Five were owned by Moy and the remainder by the SR. (R. Shephard collection)

8. There were 23 4-wheeled goods vehicles, of which two were flat and two were covered vans, as illustrated. Most goods vehicles were grey, except the vans which were maroon and the Moy wagons. The latter were red-oxide in later years. (K. Nunn collection/LCGB)

HALESWORTH.

Nine miles distant from Southwold, is a thriving market town on a tributary of the river Blyth. The fine old Church, a Gothic building is the chief object of interest to visitors. A market is held every Tuesday.

9. No. 3 arrives with the 10.55 train from Southwold on 10th September 1910, which includes one of the flat wagons, three of the wagons with raised ends to support tarpaulins and both of the company's vans. On the right are the busy sidings of the GER. (K. Nunn/LCGB)

The 25" scale map of 1904 shows the Southwold Railway on the right of the Great Eastern double track and the footbridge linking the three platforms. There is unfortunately no distinction made between narrow and standard gauge lines but this will become apparent in the following photographs.

10. Taken a few minutes after the previous photograph, no. 3 turns round its train but blocks our view of the SR station. On the left a GER engine arrives on the down line whilst an up passenger train stands under the foot-bridge. (K. Nunn/LCGB)

SOUTHWOLD and HALESWORTH (1st and 3rd class).—Southwold.
Secretary, H. Ward.   Chairman, A. C. Pain.

Up.		Week Days.							
	mrn	mrn	aft	aft	aft				
Southwold..........dep.	7 30	10 55	2 20	5 25	7 10				
Walberswick.......[ford	7 33	10 58	2 23	5 28	7 13				
Blythburgh, for Wang-	7 45	11 10	2 35	5 40	7 25				
Wenhaston...........	7 56	11 21	2 46	5 51	7 36				
Halesworth 288,292 ar	8 7	11 32	2 57	6 2	7 47				
292 London(L'poolSt.)a	11	3 30	6 09 25						

	Miles	Down.		Week Days.						
		Liverpool Street.	mrn	mrn	mrn	aft	aft			
	—	288 London..........dep.	5 5	10 0	11 45	3 25	5 0			
	—	Halesworth ......dep.	8 40	1 23	3 20	6 23	7 53			
	2¼	Wenhaston.......[ford	8 49	1 21	3 29	6 32	8 2			
	5	Blythburgh, for Wang-	9 0	1 32	3 40	6 43	8 13			
	8	Walberswick..........	9 14	1 46	3 54	6 57	8 27			
	9	Southwold..........arr.	9 17	1 49	3 57	7 0	8 30			

n Arrives at 10 45 mrn. on Mondays.

Bradshaw 1910

11. Whilst reversing at the south end of the station on 17th January 1920, the driver stares at the ground-level photographer. In the background are coaches still retaining their open end verandahs. A programme of renovation and enclosing the ends took place between 1919 and 1923. (K. Nunn/LCGB)

12. A few minutes later, no. 1 propelled the single wagon back onto its train, which was to be the 3.40 pm departure for Southwold. It seems to be still losing steam from the injector overflow. (K. Nunn/LCGB)

13. A well known postcard action shot of an evening train arriving. Notice the wooden boarded platform surface which eliminated the mud but made for difficulty in frosty weather. (Lens of Sutton)

CHEAP EXCURSION TICKETS

Will be issued to

SOUTHWOLD

Every Monday and Thursday

Stations.		Times.		Fares for Double Journey.	
		a.m.	p.m.	1 Class.	3 Class.
Halesworth	dep.	8 40	1 15	2/-	1/-
Wenhaston	,,	8 49	1 24	1/6	9 d.
Blythburgh	,,	9 0	1 35	1/-	6d.
Southwold	arr.	9 17	1 52	—	—

The Tickets will be available for Return on day of issue only from Southwold by the 5.25 p.m. during May and the 5.25 and 7.13 p.m. Trains during June.

14. With drain cocks open and a full head of steam, no. 1 starts away with the 6.30 pm to the coast as the shadows lengthen on 3rd July 1920. What locomotive elegance!
(K. Nunn/LCGB)

15. A battered but interesting photograph of the goods transfer shed. The shunting horses could, for example, move wagons over the crossover on the left and bring up more vans to the stage for the laborious operation of transhipment.
(Dr. I.C. Allen/A.B. Jenkins collection)

16. No. 2 about to enter the transfer shed with an unidentifiable load. The undated sepia photograph clearly shows that the dome was well polished. Two permanent transhippers were employed full time. (R. Shephard collection)

9th July, 1923, and until further notice.

UP TRAINS. WEEK DAYS.								SUNDAYS
		a.m.	a.m.	noon	p.m.	p.m.	p.m.	p.m.
JTHWOLD	dep.	7.30	9.45	12.0	2.20	5.23	7.26	5.19
LBERSWICK	,,	7.35	9.50	12.5	2.25	5.28	7.31	5.24
YTHBURGH	,,	7.49	10.4	12.19	2.39	5.42	7.45	5.38
NHASTON	,,	8.0	10.15	12.30	2.50	5.53	7.56	5.49
LESWORTH	arr.	8.11	10.26	12.41	3.1	6.4	8.7	6.0

DOWN TRAINS. WEEK DAYS.								SUNDAYS
		a.m.	a.m.	p.m.	p.m.	p.m.	p.m.	p.m.
LESWORTH	dep.	8.40	10.45	1.0	3.45	6.37	8.12	8.0
NHASTON	,,	8.51	10.56	1.11	3.56	6.48	8.23	8.11
YTHBURGH	,,	9.2	11.7	1.22	4.7	6.59	8.34	8.22
LBERSWICK	,,	9.15	11.20	1.35	4.20	7.12	8.47	8.35
JTHWOLD	arr.	9.21	11.26	1.41	4.26	7.18	8.53	8.41

17. An undated snap of no. 4 proceeding towards the transhipment shed, also showing the up main line platform in the foreground. (A.R. Taylor collection)

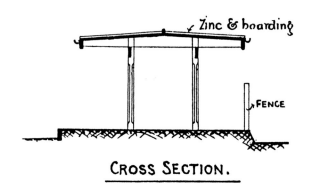

Zinc & boarding

FENCE

CROSS SECTION.

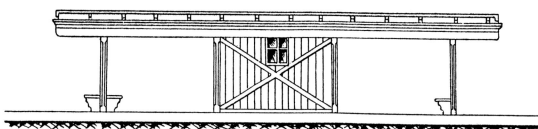

ELEVATION TO RAILWAY.

18. The continual transfer of coal by shovel from main line to narrow gauge wagons was not normally thought worthy of a photograph. However, it became newsworthy during the General Strike of 1926 and was recorded on film. The signal box is due for closure in 1985. (D.R. Lee collection)

| Sec., H. Carne.] | HALESWORTH and SOUTHWOLD.—Southwold. | [Man. Director, A. C. Pain. |

Fares	Up.	mrn	mrn	aft	aft	aft				Fares	Down.	mrn	aft	aft	aft	aft			
1 cl. 3 cl.	Southwold dep	7 30	1045	2 20	5 25	7 15	....	....	....	1 cl. 3 cl.	Halesworth dep	9 7	1 53	2 8	6 33	8 0	....	....	....
0 10 1	Walberswick a	7 33	1048	2 23	5 28	7 18	....	....	....	0 6 0 2½	Wenhaston a	9 16	1 14	3 37	6 42	8 9	....	....	....
0 8 0 4	Blythburgh * a	7 45	11 0	2 35	5 40	7 30	....	....	....	0 10 0 5	Blythburgh * a	9 27	1 25	3 48	6 53	8 20	....	....	....
1 0 0 6½	Wenhaston a	7 56	1111	2 46	5 51	7 41	....	....	....	1 4 0 8	Walberswick a	9 41	1 39	4 2	7 7	8 34	....	....	....
1 6 0 9	Haleswrth 136	8 7	1122	2 57	6 2	7 52	....	....	....	1 6 0 9	Southwold ..arr	9 44	1 42	4 5	7 10	8 37	....	....	....

☞ All 1 & 3 class.   a Stop by signal to take up, and set down on informing the Guard.   * Station for Wangford.

Bradshaw 1890

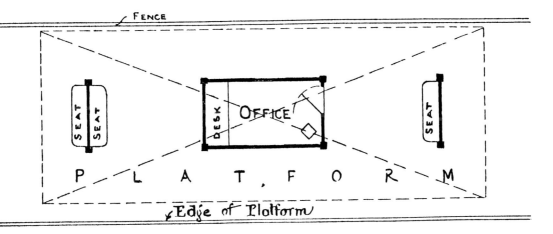

19. Holton Road with the SR bridge in the distance. Beyond it is the roof of the malthouse, partly obscured by a departing train. (R. Shephard collection)

20. A close view of the novel platform gates. The roof on the left is of the main LNER station. (R. Shephard collection)

21. Halesworth as it might have been, showing a transporter wagon in the foreground onto which loaded standard gauge wagons could be shunted. It is in fact Waterhouses, on the 2'6" gauge LMS Manifold Valley Railway in Staffordshire and was photographed by Mr. Shephard to illustrate his first revival scheme. (R. Shephard)

THE SOUTHWOLD RAILWAY A BUSY DAY AT HALESWORTH STATION - COALING UP & OVERHAULING ENGINE FOR THE RETURN JOURNEY - THE SIGNAL BEING OUT OF ORDER CAUSES MUCH DELAY.

22. Now four pictures taken on a grey September day in 1930, by Mr. Shephard, at the time when he was actively attempting to revive the line. The footbridge still connected with the two main line platforms and the exchange sidings for bulk traffic were still useable, although the SR siding is barely discernible through the grass.

23. The LNER goods shed, on the left, is on the far side of the main line. The road up to the joint goods yard is in the foreground. The overgrown track to Southwold is on the right, with the coal storage shed in the middle.

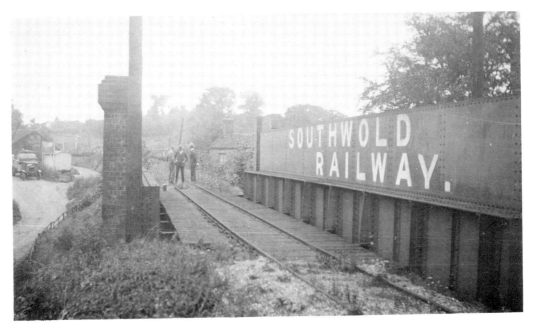

24. As the main line bridge over the Holton Road was less than 50 yards to the left of this one, the directors of the SR had taken the opportunity of advertising the existence of their railway to travellers on the LNER. Their bridge was eventually removed about 1962.

25. Turning the camera round at the same point we see the lines converging before they diverge, near the signal in the distance. Note the telephone poles carrying the uninsulated wires, common in those days, and still to be found around Lowestoft.

26. Our prospective preservationist returned five years later to find the stock unmoved and the scene unchanged. At least the sun was shining but the tarmac had worn thin.

27. Beyond the footbridge, he found that the transfer sidings were still in use, but then only for milk tankers to the nearby dairy. A few boards had fallen from the silent shed but the window glass remained intact.

28. He photographed the company's two cottages and, in his 1941 report, stated that one yielded 1/6 and the other 2/- per week rent (7½p and 10p). He also mentioned that the local council considered them unfit for habitation but they continued to be occupied until demolished in about 1960. They are marked FW on the map.

29. As World War II approached, nature reclaimed the track and one or two windows were tentatively smashed. Intending passengers were better off with a bicycle.
(G. Driver/Lens of Sutton)

30. Never mind the windows. No one seemed to own the coaches so they were regarded as a good home by a tramp. When they burnt out, arson was suspected. At least we can see the quality of the upholstery, once offered to first-class passengers. (R. Shephard)

31. This sad view has the consolation of revealing the type of vertical brake handwheel that had replaced the horizontal cranked type; once visible on the open verandahs . (R. Shephard)

32. Returning again in 1942, after another preservation attempt, this illegal war-time photograph by Ronald Shephard shows an LNER class J15 shunting, whilst the SR van has been trapped in its siding by a healthy ballast-loving shrub.

33. Each platform gate weighed about seven tons and on busy summer Saturdays had to be opened and closed up to 100 times. The smallest member of staff had to crawl inside them to oil the wheels. The station buildings remain intact today, despite being unstaffed. (P. Punchard collection)

34. Small platforms on wheels were provided in place of wicket gates for the use of pedestrians and cyclists whilst the platform gates were being opened. Peter Punchard is seen completing the platform, ready for the arrival of an up train. The installation was rendered redundant when a road bridge was built across the cutting in the distance. (P. Punchard collection)

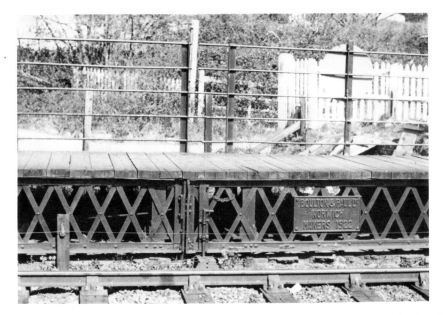

35. The 1922 maker's plate indicates that it is not the original structure. That was provided in 1888. The road surface has gone but the securing bolts remain. The last regular loco-motive hauled train ran on 11th May 1984, so that this curious platform is no longer needed.

(Both V. Mitchell)

36. The elegant down side buildings have altered little over the years. The Morris 8 is no clue to the date of the photograph. It was taken on 15th August 1984.

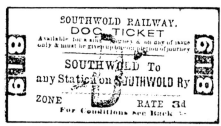

37. During the decade after closure, Ronald Shephard took various views of Halesworth locomotive shed. This 1935 shot shows the single engine accommodation erected in 1914, when the fourth engine arrived.

38. By 1936, the doors and some cladding had gone, revealing No. 3 languishing inside. The siding used to be unlocked by an Annetts key, attached to the train staff.

39. A siding had been laid at this site in 1906 to serve a railway-owned gravel pit. The shed road branched off it. Here we look towards Halesworth, at the point where the line to Southwold started to run in an easterly direction.

The Southwold Railway Company have a quantity of good gravel for disposal at the following rates:—

At WENHASTON STATION	}	
„ BLYTHBURGH „	}	4/- per ton.
„ WALBERSWICK „	}	
„ SOUTHWOLD „	}	5/- „

Applications may be made to the Station Masters, or to the Manager of the Company.

---

40. The building materials were removed for other purposes during WWII, leaving poor no. 3 to die a slow death.

41. Behind the engine shed was a chain pump, which had been installed in 1909 to supply engine water during the bridge re-building programme.

42. No. 1 hurries away from Halesworth with the 3.40 on 3rd July 1920, past a fresh crop of lineside hay. The lengthy chimney was a charming feature of SR engines. (K. Nunn/LCGB)

WENHASTON.

Six-and-a-half miles distant from Southwold. It possesses an ancient Church, in which, during the restoration in 1892, a very remarkable picture of the "Doom or Last Judgment" was discovered. The picture has been hung in the Church, and can be seen at any time. Some very good fishing can be obtained close to the station. Fishing tickets may be had of the station master

Ruins of Mells Chapel	Distance from Station 1½ miles.
Mill Heath	,, ,, ½ mile.

43. ¾ mile before reaching the station the line crossed over a short length of canal, built to bypass Wenhaston Mill. Close by was the third lock above tidal waters. Photo date – 20th November 1939. (R. Shephard)

44. Immediately after crossing the canal, the track passed over the River Blyth whose waters powered the mill in the background. Note the lack of handrails for staff safety. The mill had its own private siding. (R. Shephard)

25" scale plan of 1904.

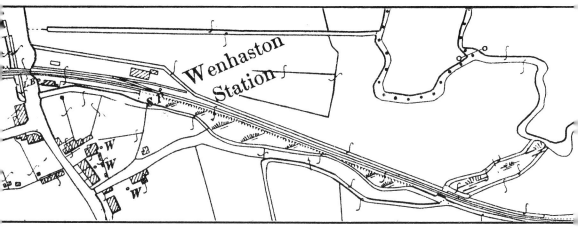

45. At the west of the station was the only public level crossing on the SR. Wicket gates were provided for pedestrians unable to wait for the road gates to be opened. Further down the road, a cart negotiates the ford across the river (a footbridge only was provided – on the left) whilst, in the distance, the canal bridge can be seen. (F. Jenkins/D. Lee)

46. The station buildings at Wenhaston, Blythburgh and Southwold were all of similar timber-framed design. Two sidings were provided. A connection to the nearest one was laid in the foreground in 1921, thus forming a loop so that wagons could be easily removed from mixed trains running in either direction. (Lens of Sutton)

47. This well known professional photograph is well worth repeating, particularly as it was taken around 1900 whilst the coaches were in their earlier livery. Note the traversing jack riding on the tank top, just in case of a derailment. (F. Jenkins)

COLLECTION AND DELIVERY OF PASSENGERS' LUGGAGE.

For the convenience of Passengers travelling from Southwold, **Special Arrangements** have been made for the Collection, Conveyance, and Delivery (within the usual limits) in London and some of the principal Provincial Towns, of Passengers' Luggage in Advance at **Cheap Rates.** Full particulars may be obtained on application at the Station.

---

48. No. 1, again, arriving with the 5.23 train from Southwold on 3rd July 1920. It includes both the company's vans and all but one of its coaches. (K. Nunn/LCGB)

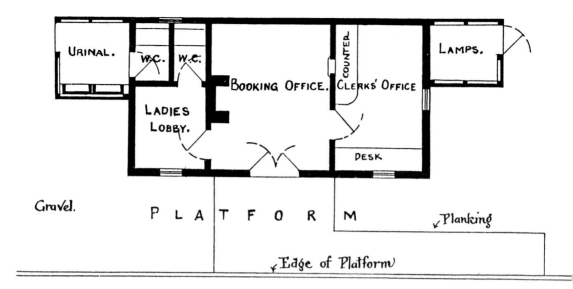

(Elevation is similar to Blythburgh Station)

URINAL.

W.C. W.C.

LADIES LOBBY.

BOOKING OFFICE.

COUNTER

CLERKS' OFFICE

DESK

LAMPS.

Gravel.

P L A T F O R M

Planking

Edge of Platform

LOADING PLATFORM

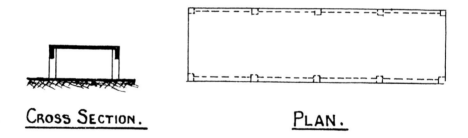

CROSS SECTION.

PLAN.

49. The generous glazing assisted in the photography of this party of Edwardian beauties. The spotty two on the right are in fact wearing netting veils attached to their headgear. The large windows and top lights would have caused the customers to cook in mid-summer and so the proprietors generously provided curtains (south side only!). (F. Jenkins/D. Lee)

50. The verandah-view of a Southwold-bound train in 1910. (K. Nunn/LCGB)

BLYTHBURGH.

Five miles distant from Southwold, contains some very fine ruins of the once famous Priory of the Augustines. The Church is also an object of considerable interest to visitors. **Dunwich** about four miles from Blythburgh, was once the capital of East Anglia, the seat of the courts of Kings, and the palaces of Bishops. The ruins of All Saints Church and a group of ivy-covered ruins of an ancient Monastery are of interest.

Walberswick Heath and Woods .. .. .. Distance from Station, 1 mile.

51. This station was not opened until three months after services had commenced. Two years later it was provided with the simple goods stage seen here and in 1908 the siding on the left was connected to the main line between the wagon and the A12 road bridge, to form a passing loop. Note the lamp with three lenses. (F. Jenkins/D.M. Lee)

SOUTHWOLD RAILWAY.

1st JANUARY. 1929, until further notice.

DOWN TRAINS.						UP TRAINS.					
	a.m.	p.m.	p.m.	p.m.			a.m.	a.m.	p.m.	p.m
Halesworth dep	8 40	1 0	3 35	6 37	Southwold dep.	7 30	9 50	2 24	5 23
Wenhaston ,,	8 51	1 11	3 46	6 48	Walberswick ,,	7 35	9 55	2 29	5 28
Blythburgh ,,	9 2	1 22	3 57	6 59	Blythburgh ,,	7 49	10 9	2 43	5 42
Walberswick ,,	9 15	1 35	4 10	7 12	Wenhaston ,,	8 0	10 20	2 54	5 53
Southwold arr.	9 21	1 41	4 16	7 18	Halesworth arr.	8 11	10 31	3 5	6 4

52. Arthur Pain, one of the engineers for the construction of the line, chose to use station building plans that he had previously used on other minor railways. They were first used on the Swindon and Highworth line (with board cladding) and later on the Culm Valley route in Devon (with brick in-filling). Here we see Uffculme, on the latter line to Hemyock. Did the directors know that they were paying for third-hand drawings? (Lens of Sutton)

53. A Halesworth-bound train rumbles under the main road bridge, whilst the driver applies the engine's brakes so that the two vans will stop by the milk churns. The coal storage shed, on the left, has a curious mixture of vertical and horizontal boarding. (R. Shephard collection)

54. A down train clatters away with the leading first compartment empty. Its door is wide open to allow engine smuts to settle on the first-class padded seats before the next well-dressed passenger descends onto it. In the background of this postcard is the cathedral-like church of this small village. (Lens of Sutton)

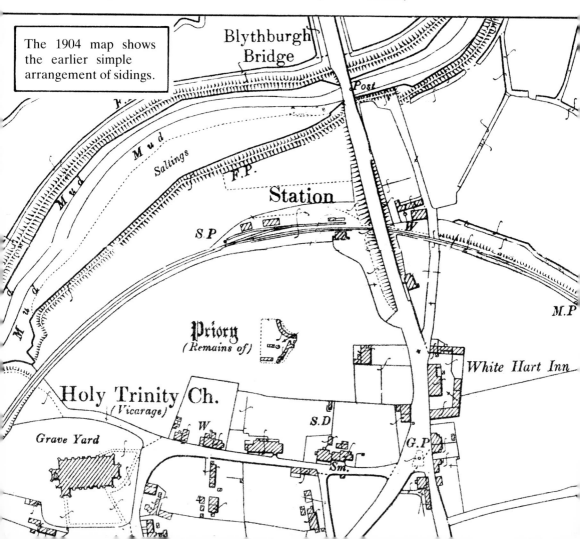

The 1904 map shows the earlier simple arrangement of sidings.

55. Milk traffic originated from Blythburgh and Wenhaston principally and was mainly destined for London. Lack of Sunday trains on the branch meant a longer working day for herdsmen on the Sabbath as they had to transport the churns by cart to the main line. (Revd E.R. Boston collection)

56. The coming of the railway to this small village broadened the horizon for the inhabitants. A trip to the high spots of Southwold became a pleasant day out, away from the rough dusty roads. The station master stands to attention with the staff in hand. (P. Punchard collection)

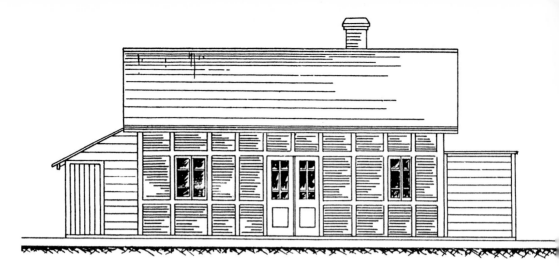

ELEVATION TO RAIL.

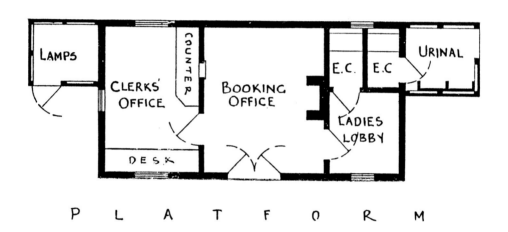

LAMPS

CLERKS' OFFICE

COUNTER

BOOKING OFFICE

E.C. E.C

URINAL

LADIES LOBBY

DESK

P L A T F O R M

Edge of Platform

Sanitation historians will like to note that the toilets were provided with ECs and not WCs.

LOADING PLATFORM

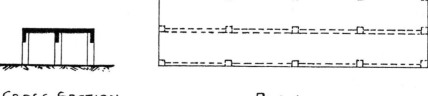

CROSS SECTION

PLAN

57. Two eastward views that were part of the Shephard 1930 survey. Here is the approach to the loop, with the bi-directional signal and both the coal and goods sheds visible. Coal was stored in the open in most railway goods yards – were these Victorian villagers coal thieves as well as smugglers?

58. The road bridge survived until 1961, by which time most of the other structures had gone. Note that the wooden platform surface had survived to the end. The level crossing in the foreground had probably been used by carts taking milk churns to the platform edge.

59. One of only two buildings to survive on the line is the coal shed, well concealed by overgrown hedges and pictured here in April 1984. (V. Mitchell)

LOCAL RATES FOR PARCELS

BY

PASSENGER TRAIN.

Between any two Stations on the Southwold Railway, including Collection and Delivery (within certain limits) at Southwold and Walberswick only.

Not exceeding 1 lb.	3D.
Over 1 lb. and not exceeding 8 lbs.	4D
For every additional 8 lbs. or part thereof	1D.

Fractions of a Penny are charged as a Penny.

Each Parcel will be charged for separately.

Parcels, to ensure their being forwarded, must be delivered at the station 15 minutes before the departure of the Trains by which they are required to be sent ; if when later they are sent on, the Company will not hold themselves responsible for any irregularities or loss occasioned by hasty despatch, nor do they undertake to forward them unless received within that time.

60. Tinkers Covert and Deadman's Covert were the unattractive names given to this attractive area, the most densely wooded part of the line. It is most pleasingly known as The Heronry. (A.B. Jenkins collection)

61. This scenic view graced the cover of the Company's 48-page timetable book (price 1d) in 1914, from which the advertisements in this album are reproduced.
(F. Jenkins/D. Lee)

The 6" to the mile scale map of 1928 showing the remoteness of the station from the village and the location of the Harbour branch. FB marks the position of the footbridge on the golf course.

WALBERSWICK.

This charming village, one mile from Southwold, will be found an attractive place for the artist, and indeed for all who have eyes for quiet beauty. The old weather-stained and ivy-clad Church is perhaps the most picturesque ruin of East Suffolk.

Ruins of Walberswick Church	..	..	..	Distance from Station, ¼ mile.
Walberswick Common	..	..	..	Adjoining Station.
Southwold Harbour	..	..	..	Distance from Station, 1¼ miles.

62. Photographed in the early 1890s, we can see a pile of fish boxes on the platform and the old swing bridge in the distance. The company minute book records that the station was opened on 2nd September 1881 but the Board of Trade records state that approval for opening was given on 1st July 1882 (despite only a urinal being provided for the convenience of passengers). (J. Martyn/D. Lee)

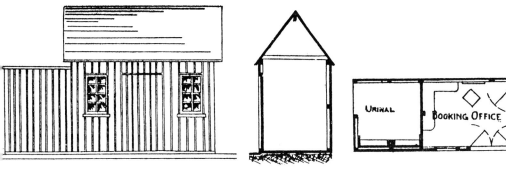

25" scale map of 1904.

63. This view can be dated 1902, as that is the
year in which the telephone system was installed and in which a larger station, with a
booking office, was built.
(F. Jenkins/A.B. Jenkins collection)

64. Little competition for the railway was
generated by the commencement of a steam
ferry service across the river. There was no
road to the station – only a bridle path, half a
mile long! The ferry operated from the end of
the village street, but there was an equally
long walk on the opposite shore.
(R. Shephard collection).

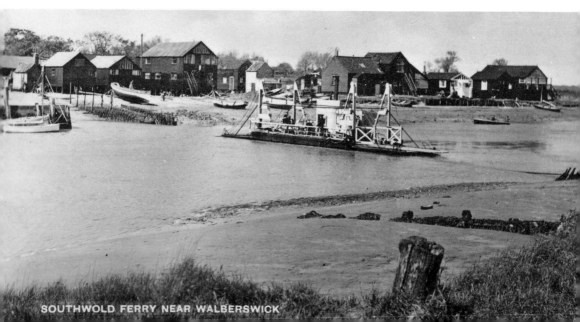

SOUTHWOLD FERRY NEAR WALBERSWICK

65. The enlarged station looking towards Southwold. Note the large coal storage shed and the pony and trap, awaiting a passenger. The station was temporarily closed on 2nd April 1917 for the duration of WWI and was demolished during WWII.
(D. Lee collection)

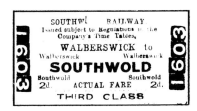

66. Two sidings were provided and were fitted with this unusual catch point, to prevent wagons accidentally running out onto the main line. The rail end was moveable in the wide chair. (R. Shephard)

67. The first bridge to be widened, after the 1906 decision to convert to standard gauge, was the swing bridge. This view shows the original fixed span (on the right) which was replaced in 1914. 1911 was the last year in which the bridge was swung open, other than for annual maintenance purposes. Between 1879 and 1894, it was only opened once. The swing span was 146 ft long and the fixed span was 73 ft 6 ins long. Despite the differences between the spans, it was an elegant feature in the landscape, particularly at high tide. (R. Shephard collection)

68. Bottoms up! In 1938 it was a difficult structure to cross on foot. Note the generous loading gauge width. (R. Shephard)

69. By 1942, the Army had rendered this fine monument to the SR quite useless – in the interests of national security. Another illegal photograph! (R. Shephard)

App. Drewett & Sons Ltd., 30, Victoria Street. S.W.

(43).

6919 Southwold Railway.

For Army, Navy, Police on Duty, etc.

No. of Ticket _____ 22. 7. 1916.

(OUTWARD JOURNEY)

From *Blythburgh* To *Catterick Bridge N.E.R.*

Via *Halesworth. G.N. & G.E. Th. York & Durham*

Description.	Class.	Number of Passengers at				Ordinary Single Fare.	Amount Payable.	
		½ Single Fare.	⅔ Single Fare.	¾ Single Fare.	Full Single Fare.			
Officers	1st	1.					19	4.
Soldiers or Sailors... ...	3rd	6.					3 .	0 . 0
Their Wives	,,							
,, Children (above 12)...	,,							
,, ,, (3 to 12 Half-fare)	,,							
Police	,,							
Others								
* Insert description. Total							3 .	19 4

Warrant No. *36 — G.R. — 2529.* _____ _____ Booking Clerk.

Through tickets in the cases where the journey is not continuous do not include the cost of transfer between Railway Termini in Towns or between Railway and Steamboats.

N.B.—This Ticket must be shown or given up when required.

70. Southwold Harbour during an exceptionally high tide, about 1936. The little used branch line is visible in the foreground, leading towards the weighbridge hut. The weighbridge was a second-hand standard gauge unit, with a third rail fitted to it. It would have been a wise purchase had the gauge conversion gone ahead and had WWI not killed off the harbour development. The barge-mounted steam crane on the right was being used for further harbour reconstruction work. (F. Jenkins/A.B. Jenkins)

71. On 29th November 1897, severe floods washed away the embankment between the bridge and Southwold Common. Trains terminated at Walberswick and passengers crossed the river in small boats. Later horse buses took them to Blythburgh.
(Revd E.R. Boston collection)

72. During that winter, it appears that the line was reconstructed on a higher embankment. Identical circumstances crippled another minor railway and are fully described in our *Branch Line to Selsey*. (A.B. Jenkins)

73. A view at the same location, showing the cutting through the Common in the distance. On the left is a gradient post (1 in 66, down from the bridge) and on the right is a milepost (8 from Halesworth). The rails were 30 lbs per yard and were laid on 6 ft x 6 ins x 3 ins sleepers. (A.B. Jenkins/D. Lee)

74. The Golf Club paid £50 for the erection of this footbridge across the cutting in the Common. It was constructed in 1904, using old rails for the main components.
(K. Nunn/LCGB)

75. Steps were provided at each end of the decking. Miss A.M. and Master F.H. Jenkins, of the well known local family, pose to allow bridge details to be photographed.
(F. Jenkins/A.B. Jenkins)

SOUTHWOLD.

The **GEM** of the East Coast, is a pretty sea-side town in Suffolk standing on a bold cliff and commanding an extensive view of the North Sea. The climate is most healthy and invigorating. It is appropriately termed "Sunny Southwold." There are miles of golden sands, also an extensive common.

The scenery round Southwold is exceptionally pretty, and the **Walks and Drives** in the neighbourhood are numerous and interesting. To the pedestrian and the cyclist the surrounding district offers many attractions.

Southwold possesses a **Good Reading Room, Circulating Library,** and plenty of **Good Hotel and Boarding House Accommodation.**

There is a **Well-built Pier** from which excellent Fishing can be obtained. The Drainage and Water Supply are both good.

Mixed Bathing is allowed.

76. One of the oldest views of the station, before it was extended. It was probably taken a few years after the opening, as boiler work is being carried out on a locomotive – its dome cover is on the ground. Ankles still could not be displayed.
(A.B. Jenkins collection)

77. Mr. J. Kumbara visited the line as a representative of the Japanese Railway Company and presented this photograph to Mr. A.E. Wright, the railway guard, on 15th November 1887. Not surprisingly, it has faded a little, after nearly a century. (Southwold Museum)

78. Probably taken in the 1890s, we see that the station has had a lean-to extension tastefully added on the left and also a carriage canopy provided over the entrance doors. The coach on the left appears to be in the original livery, whilst the others are in cream. Note the opening top lights. (F. Jenkins/A.B. Jenkins)

TOURIST, FORTNIGHTLY,

AND

FRIDAY to TUESDAY TICKETS

FROM

LONDON

ARE ISSUED AS UNDER BY ALL TRAINS TO

SOUTHWOLD.

TOURIST. A		FORTNIGHTLY, Available for 15 days. B		FRIDAY OR SATURDAY TILL TUESDAY. C	
FIRST CLASS.	THIRD CLASS.	FIRST CLASS.	THIRD CLASS.	FIRST CLASS.	THIRD CLASS.
31/3	18/5	27/6	15/-	22/-	11/-

A—Tourist Tickets are issued by any Train on any day, and are avaliable for return by any of the advertised Trains on any day within Six Calendar Months.

B—Fortnightly Tickets are issued by any Train on any day, and are available for return by any of the advertised Trains on any day within 15 days, including the days of issue and return.

C—Friday to Tuesday Tickets are issued every Friday or Saturday by any Train, and are available for return by any of the advertised Trains on the day of issue, or on any day (Sunday if Train service permits) up to and including the Tuesday following.

We may think that British Rail's ticketing systems are complicated but it is not new!

79. This postcard was produced soon after 1900, when the Station Hotel was erected. It dwarfed the modest station. Notice the simple buffer stop at the end of the siding and the cart belonging to Mr. Doy, the company's cartage agent. (Lens of Sutton)

W. DOY, (Cartage Agent for Southwold Railway),

CARTER,

15 LORNE ROAD, SOUTHWOLD.

Luggage Cart Meets all Trains.

MILK & CREAM DELIVERED DAILY.

80. The scene, in about 1902, includes an iron vat destined for Adnams Brewery. It seems to be in excess of loading gauge although the original swing bridge could accommodate a load 11 ft wide. The lean-to had been replaced by a full scale extension. (F. Jenkins/D. Lee)

81. A fine display of Edwardian luggage, with W. Doy's cart at the ready. Holiday travel at its best. Note the now-extinct port-manteaux on the left and the obligatory hat box on VDH's trunk in the middle. (F. Jenkins/D. Lee)

1904 map to the scale 25" to the mile.

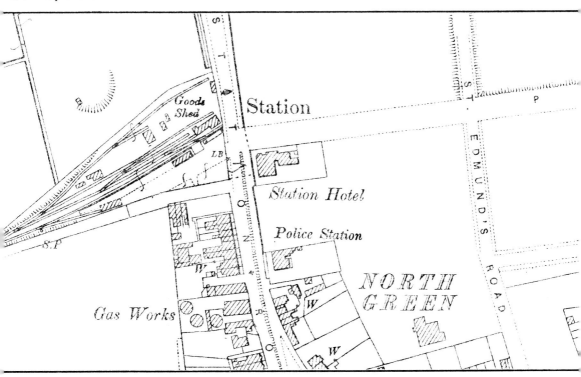

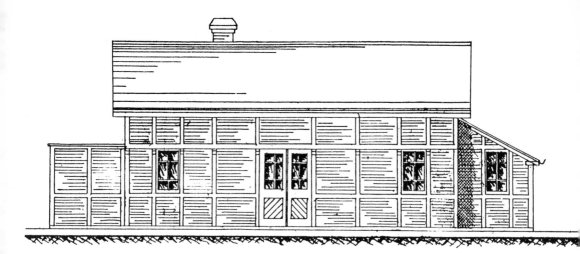

ELEVATION TO RAIL.

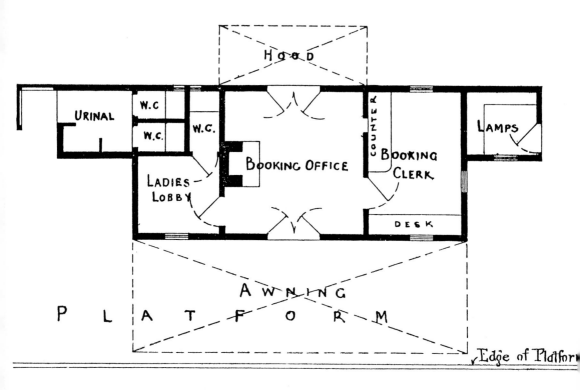

CHEAP WEEK-END and **LONG-DATE TICKETS** are issued from some of the principal Stations on the Midland, London and North Western, North Eastern, Great Northern, and Great Central Railways to

SOUTHWOLD.

FULL PARTICULARS CAN BE OBTAINED AT THE STATION OR FROM THE MANAGER.

82. The platform oil lamps were displaced by electric lights in 1905, so that this post card had been in stock some time when it was franked – 8.15 pm May 20th 1913. Don't miss the vintage perambulator, mail-cart or baby carriage. (A.B. Jenkins collection)

83. No. 3 *Blyth* shunts a well laden Cleminson wagon, circa 1908. Wagons were often shunted by hand, particularly between the goods shed and the train. (F. Jenkins/D. Lee)

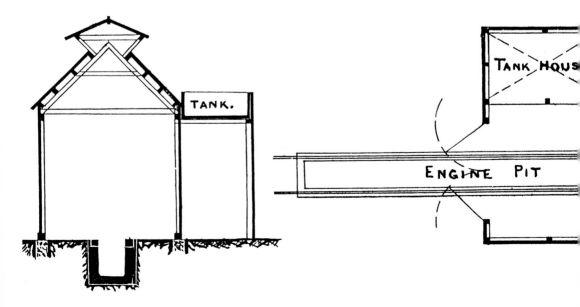

TANK.

TANK HOUSE

ENGINE PIT

84. A rare view of the small goods platform and shed at the end of the line, with no. 3 on the run round loop. Great Eastern poster boards are behind the seats and the weighing machine is set into the platform, outside the parcel office door.
(Revd E.R. Boston collection)

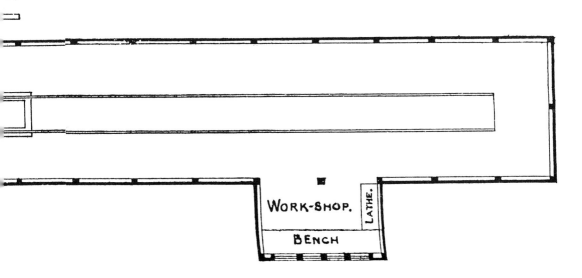

P.

WORK-SHOP. LATHE.

BENCH

85. Gravel predominated as the platform surface but the far side had been decked with wood. No wonder hat boxes were needed on holiday. (Lens of Sutton)

86. Six views taken in 1910-11 by Ken Nunn. *Blyth* (in steam) stands beside *Halesworth*, whose rear cab doors are displayed clearly. These were provided to facilitate the use of long-handled fire irons. Note that the engines face opposite directions and change direction during the course of this book. They were probably turned whilst away at Stratford Works.

87. No. 3 waits for the right-away as the evening shadows lengthen. The second wagon appears to have no brakes.

IPSWICH

Every Monday,

AS UNDER :—

Stations.					Times.		Fares for the Double Journey.	
					a.m.	a.m.	1 Cl.	3 Cl.
Southwold	dep.				7 30	10 50		
Walberswick	,,				7 35	10 55		
Blythburgh	,,				7 45	11 5	6/6	3/3
Wenhaston	,,				7 56	11 16		
Ipswich	arr.				9 1	1 22	—	—

Available for Return on day of issue only from Ipswich at 6.38 p.m.

88. No. 1 is up on blocks whilst its wheels were away for re-profiling or re-tyreing. There was no wheel lathe on the railway. In front of it, the entrance gate to the yard can be seen. The fitter is preparing no. 3 for the road.

89. No. 3 "ready for the road". A can of cylinder oil stands by the smokebox, the heat from which kept it sufficiently viscous to pour into the nearby lubricator. The yard was the scene of prolonged laborious shovelling – look between the smokeboxes.

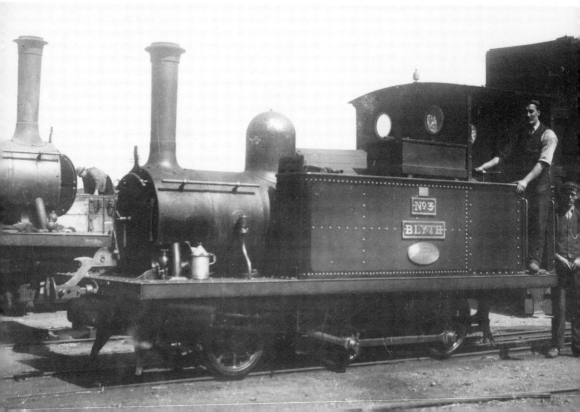

90. Looking at the throat of the goods yard we see various wheel sets scattered around. Even with a number of Cleminson vehicles in use, wheel wear was a problem, no doubt aggravated by the sand blown onto the track, particularly near the estuary. The carriage shed on the right was built in stages from old rails from about 1903, although it had been authorised by the Board in 1888.

Cheap Return Tickets

TO

LONDON (LIVERPOOL STREET.)

| | | FARES for the Double Journey. | |
FROM		FIRST CLASS.	THIRD CLASS.
SOUTHWOLD	... ...	27/2	12/4
WALBERSWICK	... ..	26/11	12/2
BLYTHBURGH	.. ...	26/3	11/10
WENHASTON	. .	25/10	11/7

The above Tickets will be available for return by any Train only on the Sunday (if Train Service permits) or Monday following the date of issue.

91 A rare chance to examine the rear details of no. 1. The chopper-type coupling necessitated a protective plate on the bunker or maybe it was a patching plate to cover the hole already made. Boards had been thoughtfully fitted to protect the cab back plate, when coaling up. They also acted as a lid to the bunker. (R. Shephard collection)

92. The departing passenger's view, circa 1912, as the well-wishers turn their backs on the train and wander away. The lamp posts seem to be in proportion to the lofty carriage shed but not to the small station. (D. Lee collection)

Extra Journey Return Tickets
at Reduced Fares

Are issued from the undermentioned Stations to Liverpool Street (not London Suburban Stations) and back, to Visitors holding not less than two tourist or Fortnightly Tickets.

FROM	EXTRA JOURNEY FARES TO LIVERPOOL STREET.	
	FIRST CLASS.	THIRD CLASS.
	S. D.	S. D.
SOUTHWOLD	**18 9**	**11 0**
WALBERSWICK		

These Cheap Return Tickets are issued to enable a member of a family to make occasional journeys, for business or other purposes, during the stay of the family at the Sea-side, and will be available for one week from the date of issue.   In the event of two members of the family requiring to make the extra journey, the production of not less than four Tourist or Fortnightly Tickets will be necessary. These tickets are not issued to Residents or to other than bona-fide Visitors who have taken up their residence for not less than one week at the Sea-side.

93. No. 4 clanks past the only signal post to bear a shunt arm and the only one to be provided with a shelter for the signalman. This was at the approach to the station. Note the weighted point lever. (P. Punchard collection)

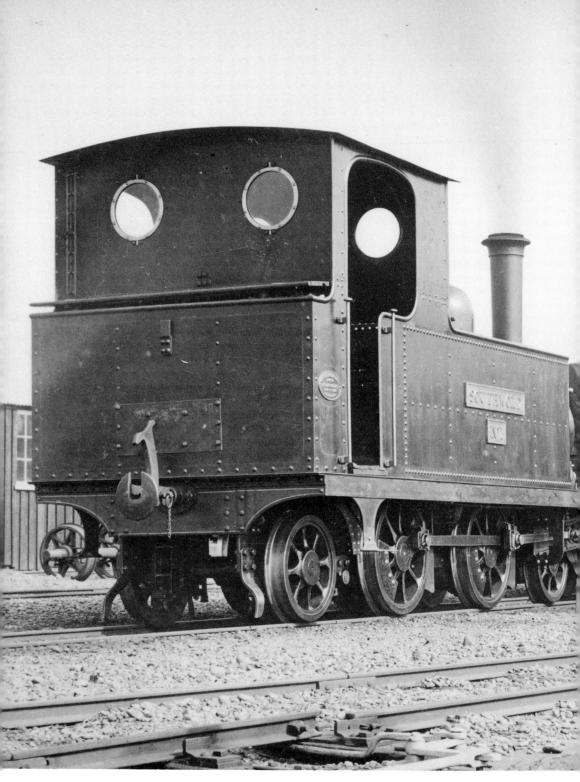

94. A number of details in this splendid photograph are worth noting. The coal bunker lid; the way in which the curved ends of the wagons helped to prevent puddles forming in the tarpaulins; and the curious catch point in the foreground.
(F. Moore/R. Shephard collection)

95. Whilst most railways in Britain used a flexible bag on their locomotive water fillers, the Southwold Railway was different, yet again, in using a foreign-style rigid curved pipe. (H.F. Hilton/Revd E.R. Boston)

96. A railwayman steps in front of the arriving train whilst Guard Wright looks at the camera. Note the fine end view of the carriage in its shed. The end doors had patterned glass. (R. Shephard collection)

97. A closer look at the well respected guard shows interesting detail of the uniform of the period and the ornate verandah roof bracket. (A.B. Jenkins collection)

98. Scrutiny of the wheel sets reveals an unusual type of bifurcated spoke. Now, a close look at the mixed train reveals that it has one more than the regulation seven goods vehicles in its composition. The second wagon appears to be carrying a large bevel gear and the leading wagon is loaded with barrels. The railway certainly was the general carrier for many years. (Lens of Sutton)

SOUTHWOLD RAILWAY.

SATURDAY TO MONDAY

IN

YARMOUTH & LOWESTOFT

EVERY SATURDAY until further notice

CHEAP RETURN TICKETS

TO

YARMOUTH and

LOWESTOFT

WILL BE ISSUED BY ANY TRAIN AT THE UNDER-MENTIONED REVISED FARES:

FROM	FARES FOR THE DOUBLE JOURNEY.			
	LOWESTOFT (C.)		YARMOUTH (S.T.)	
	First Class	Third Class	First Class	Third Class
SOUTHWOLD	4/8	2/11	7/6	3/4

The above Tickets will be available for return by any Train only on the Sunday (if train Service permits) or Monday following the date of issue.

A similar arrangement is in force *from* Yarmouth and Lowestoft **to** SOUTHWOLD.

99. This June 1920 view shows the Station Hotel of 1900 and the Southwold Hosiery Co's factory of 1909 on the left. The length of the engine shed and the extent of the coal yard are more apparent from the air than in ground level photographs.
(R. Shephard collection)

100. Holiday traffic jams are not a new phenomenon. Only the smell has changed – from horse dung to petrol exhaust. In the background, the train arrives: in the foreground, the gipsies arrive with their baskets of lace and pegs for sale. Compare the size of the station with the one in the photograph no. 78. (Lens of Sutton)

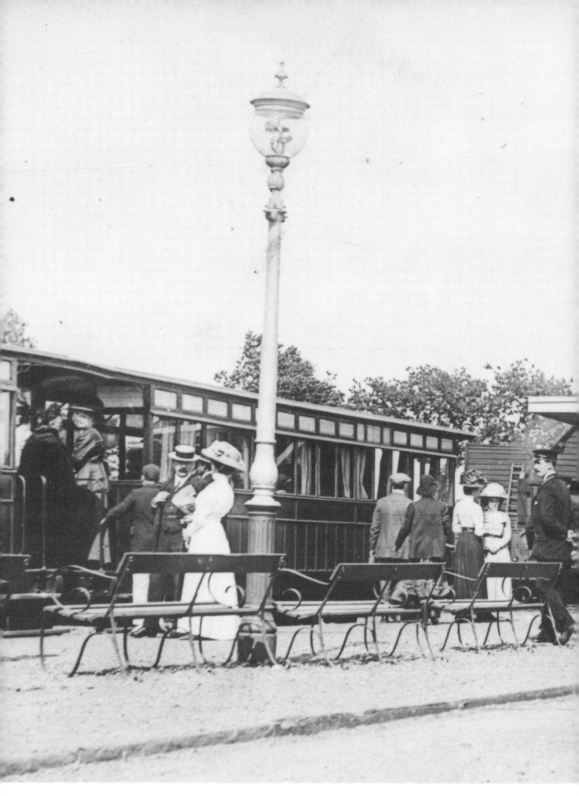

101. Not an uncovered head in sight. The station was one of the important places in the town where it was imperative to be seen to be properly dressed. Notice the lack of fencing and ticket barriers. The "open" station principle is now beginning to be adopted by British Rail. (Lens of Sutton)

102. The two vans must have covered a higher mileage than any other SR vehicle. They appear together in so many photographs. Ales and mails; hat boxes and fish boxes; prams and rams; they served the community well. (Lens of Sutton)

103. Eastern Counties Road Car Co. buses and the advent of private motoring brought about the decline of this lovable railway byway. This specimen was photographed at Southwold in about 1929, complete with a security box for the Royal Mail. (A.B. Jenkins collection)

104. The cladding of the carriage shed was carried out in stages as funds allowed but doors were never fitted. It was therefore of limited benefit to the coaches, particularly in swirling snow. (Revd E.R. Boston collection)

THE SOUTHWOLD RAILWAY – WAITING AT THE TERMINUS FOR THE DOWN EXPRESS WHICH IS SOMEWHAT LATE - A VERY UNUSUAL OCCURRENCE.

105. Road transport 1920s style. As there was no platform fence, goods traffic was often transferred here as the goods platform and shed were very small and frequently congested. (Revd E.R. Boston collection)

Southwold Railway.

SEASON TICKET.

No. ....

THIRD CLASS.

ISSUED TO

....

AVAILABLE BETWEEN

....

....

Expires ....

NOT TRANSFERABLE.

And subject to the conditions of the Agreement between the Holder and the Southwold Railway Co.

H. WARD,

Manager and Secretary.

107. There were insufficient doors left to put any on the north side. It did not matter because, like the Tal-y-Llyn Railway, there were no platforms on that side in any case. But you could still travel to Tollesbury, in Essex, on a verandah if you were so inclined. (R. Shephard)

106. During the carriage rebuilding programme in 1918 to 1923, the verandahs were covered in and the end doors moved to the sides. This less attractive arrangement was worsened by the provision of new dissimilar handrails. The driver seems weary. Nos. 1 and 4 were more comfortable for the crew, as they had one more axle than nos. 2 and 3. (Lens of Sutton)

108. No. 25 was one of the first batch of SR 6-wheelers and was built in 1896. No. 1 was one of the first batch of 4-wheelers and was built in 1879. Both had survived to the end when this and the previous photograph were taken in 1929. Notice the coal cart shafts pointing heaven-wards. (R. Shephard)

110. Five photographs of the last week of operation, loaned by Mr. Barrett Jenkins. Some of the staff pose in a goods wagon, at the end of the line, in both senses of the phrase. The trellis fence, behind the weighing machine, is the boundary with Station Road.

109. The blast pipes lying on the buffer beam remind us of the continual battle with boiler corrosion that has to be fought on every steam railway. On the right of the engine shed is the locomotive water filler and, further to the right, the short goods platform. (Revd E.R. Boston collection)

111. Operating staff pose for their farewell photograph. Stationmaster Girling gives the official handshakes to the footplate crew.

ALDEBURGH

Every Week-day,

AS UNDER :—

Stations.			Times.			Fares for the Double Journey.	
			a.m.	a.m.		1 Cl.	3 Cl.
Southwold ... . dep.			7 30	10 50	...		
Walberswick ... ... „			7 35	10 55	...	5/6	2/9
Aldeburgh ... ... arr.			11 38	1 14	...		

Available for return on day of issue only from Aldeburgh at 4.25 p.m. during May and 6.45 p.m. during June.

112. From left to right – Mr George Burley, an unknown cyclist, Mr Bert Girling (Station Master), Mr Aldous, Mr George Self and Mr Barrett Jenkins, with cine camera in hand.

113. One of the last passengers to travel on the last train was Major Debney (on the left), who had also travelled on the first train, 50 years earlier. In front of him is Mr J.S. Hurst, Borough Surveyor of that time.

114. Stop – for ever. For economy, the two signal arms had been mounted on a single post. For further economy, a single oil lamp with two lenses was used between the coloured spectacle glasses. For economy of effort, the lamp was hoisted by a cable running over a pulley and operated by a winch at the base of the post. Thus the need to climb ladders was obviated. (R. Shephard)

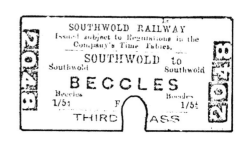

SOUTHWOLD RAILWAY
Issued subject to Regulations in the
Company's Time Tables.
SOUTHWOLD to
Southwold   Southwold
BECCLES
Beccles   Beccles
1/5½   F   1/5½
THIRD   ASS

115. By 1933, the coal heaps had spread and buses stood in the station approach. The lamp winch and signal levers are visible and the spectacle frames are more obvious.
(R. Shephard collection)

116. By 1939, much of the boarding of the water tower had been stolen, but this made it look more like a water tower. The goods shed (on the right) had been turned through 90° in about 1912. The engine shed was blown down in 1942. (R. Shephard)

117. The same year, wheeled beach huts had been parked in the yard whilst coastal defence work was in progress. The preservationist was still undeterred. (R. Shephard)

119. One of the van bodies inexplicably found itself being used as a tool shed on an allotment. When discovered by Mr Barrett Jenkins in 1962, it was moved back to the station site. It is seen here at the eastern end of the station (the toilets of which had been demolished). In 1968, it was moved to the East Anglian Transport Museum at Carlton Colville, near Lowestoft. (A.B. Jenkins)

118. The Austin 7 and Morris 12 give the impression of a pre-war photograph, but it was taken in 1960. Then came stations of a different sort. In 1965, a new fire station was built in the coal yard and, in 1968, the building illustrated was demolished, to make way for a new police station. (R. Shephard)

120. The goods shed was moved yet again. It now resides at the west end of the station site, in Blyth Road, and is used by the Southwold Allotment Holders Association whose plots are located on part of the former railway route. To paraphrase a saying known to many medical students – the Southwold Railway never died, it only faded away. (V. Mitchell)

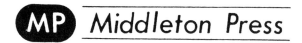

MP *Middleton Press*

Easebourne Lane, Midhurst, West Sussex, GU29 9AZ
☎ Midhurst (073 081) 3169